THE KENT & EAST RAILWAY
by Jonathan James

Front Cover No.14 Charwelton working the 09:56 Bodiam to Tenterden Town at the bottom of Tenterden Bank during the Spring Gala on 2 May 2011.

Phil Barnes

Back Cover 30065 Maunsell shunting at Bodiam on 17 July 2016.

Jonathan James

Above Single line tokens are exchanged as No. 25 arrives at Wittersham Road on 16 June 2019.

Phil Barnes

Published by Mainline & Maritime Ltd
3 Broadleaze, Upper Seagry, near Chippenham, SN15 5EY
Tel: 07770 748615
www.mainlineandmaritime.co.uk   orders@mainlineandmaritime.co.uk
Printed in the UK
ISBN: 978-1-900340-80-9
©Mainline & Maritime Ltd & Jonathan James 2020
All rights reserved. No part of this publication may be reproduced by any process without the prior written permission of the publisher.

INTRODUCTION

Growing up, my summer holidays were often taken at Camber Sands in East Sussex, which resulted in an early introduction to the Kent and East Sussex Railway. My first visit was not long after the railway reopened in 1974, when it ran between Tenterden and Rolvenden. I remember returning a few years later, by which time the railway had been extended to Wittersham Road, providing a much longer journey.

I have visited several times since to enjoy a gentle journey through the Kent countryside and a visit to Bodiam Castle. The railway now serves five stations and there are plans to extend the line through to Robertsbridge, which will provide a main line connection. The extension project is being managed by the Rother Valley Railway. Despite the expansion of the railway, it has retained a quiet charm, which really does take you back in time to the days of 'Hop Pickers Specials' and a much calmer pace of life.

I would like to thank Mike Smith and Phil Barnes for providing some photographs for this book, along with Iain McCall at Mainline and Maritime for his help and advice.

I hope you enjoy reading this book and that it will inspire you to visit the railway and enjoy the surrounding countryside and attractions.

Jonathan James, July 2020

'Terrier' 32670 has steam to spare as it passes the Sports Centre grounds at Robertsbridge on the Rother Valley Railway, on the occasion of the 'Return To Steam' Gala on 22 September 2013.

Phil Barnes

THE KENT & EAST SUSSEX RAILWAY

The Rother Valley Railway opened in 1900 between Robertsbridge and Tenterden (now called Rolvenden). The railway was built as a light railway and followed the Rother Valley, a route which required minimal engineering. H.F. Stephens was appointed engineer and later went on to become the Managing Director. In 1903 an extension opened from Tenterden to Tenterden Town and the original Tenterden station was renamed Rolvenden.

The South Eastern and Chatham Railway, meanwhile started work on constructing the line between Tenterden Town and Headcorn, although the railway would continue to be operated by the Rother Valley Railway. This section of line was engineered to a higher standard and included a short tunnel near Tenterden St Michael's. The Tenterden Town to Headcorn section opened in 1905, by which time the Rother Valley Railway had been renamed the Kent and East Sussex Railway.

After leaving the mainline at Robertsbridge, trains called at Junction Road, Bodiam, Northiam, Wittersham Road, Rolvenden, Tenterden Town, Tenterden St Michael's, High Halden Road, Biddenden, Frittenden Road and finally Headcorn, which also provided a main line connection. A further halt opened at Salehurst, between Robertsbridge and Junction Road, in 1903.

Tenterden Town was the most significant station on the line and at one point had three platforms. The railway carried a reasonable amount of passenger and freight traffic, with 105,676 passengers carried in 1913. The line conveyed a variety of goods traffic including livestock. Passenger and goods traffic slowly declined until World War II, when the railway was used as the base for two rail mounted guns and was also used as a diversionary route for other rail traffic.

In 1948 the railway became part of British Railways and a modest programme of enhancements commenced, however traffic continued to decline and in 1954 all regular passenger traffic ceased and the line between Tenterden and Headcorn closed completely. Hop Pickers specials continued until 1958, along with the occasional enthusiasts special and the remaining freight traffic between Tenterden and Robertsbridge. By 1961 the only remaining traffic was between Robertsbridge and Hodson's Flour Mill just outside Robertsbridge, which eventually ceased in 1970.

Not long after the railway closed, a preservation society was formed, which concentrated on reopening the line between Tenterden Town and Bodiam. A separate organisation, the Rother Valley Railway, was later formed to reopen the line between Bodiam and Robertsbridge. The railway has reopened as follows:
• Tenterden Town to Rolvenden – 1974;
• Rolvenden to Wittersham Road - 1977 (the station opened in 1978);
• Wittersham Road to Northiam – 1990;
• Northiam to Bodiam - 2000 (although occasional shuttles operated between Dixter Halt and Bodiam between 1981 and 1983);
• Bodiam to Junction Road - 2011 (occasional operation only);
• Robertsbridge to Northbridge Street - 2011 (occasional operation only).

The section between Northbridge Street and Junction Road is being reconstructed by the Rother Valley Railway, although no firm opening date has been confirmed, pending a Transport and Works Act application.

The Class 108 DMU waits to depart from Bodiam with the 15:15 service for Tenterden on 3 July 2011.

Phil Barnes

TRACK PLANS

Not to scale

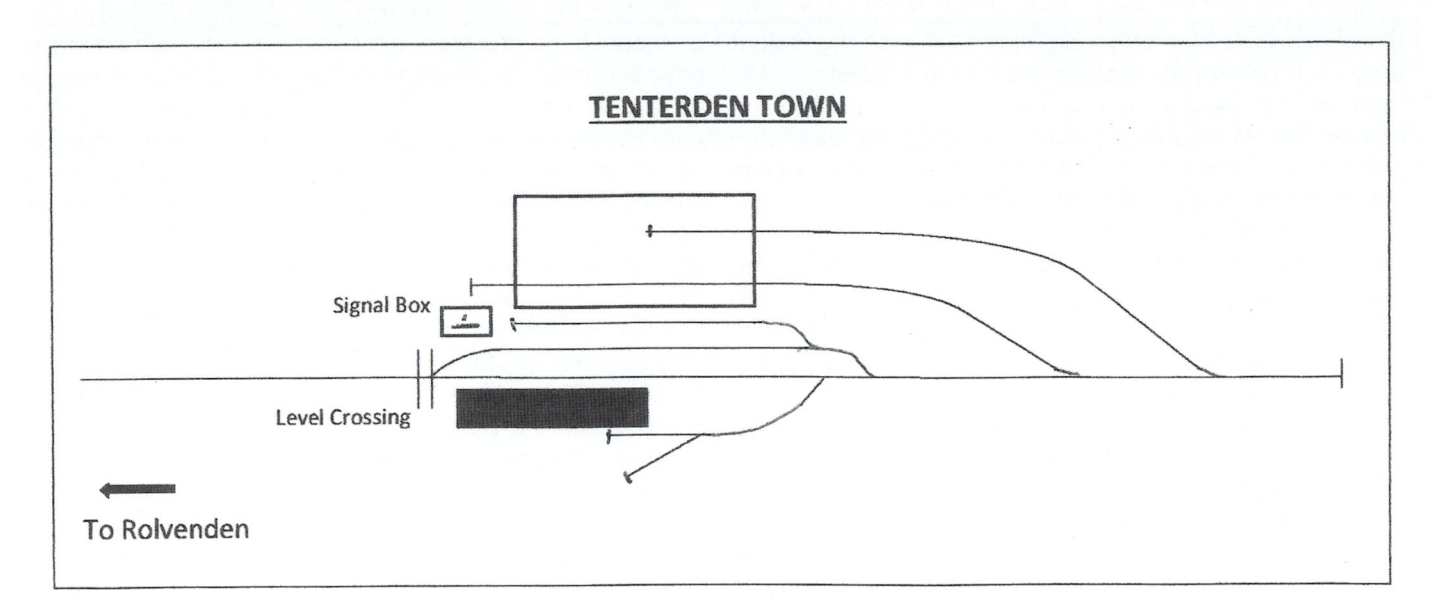

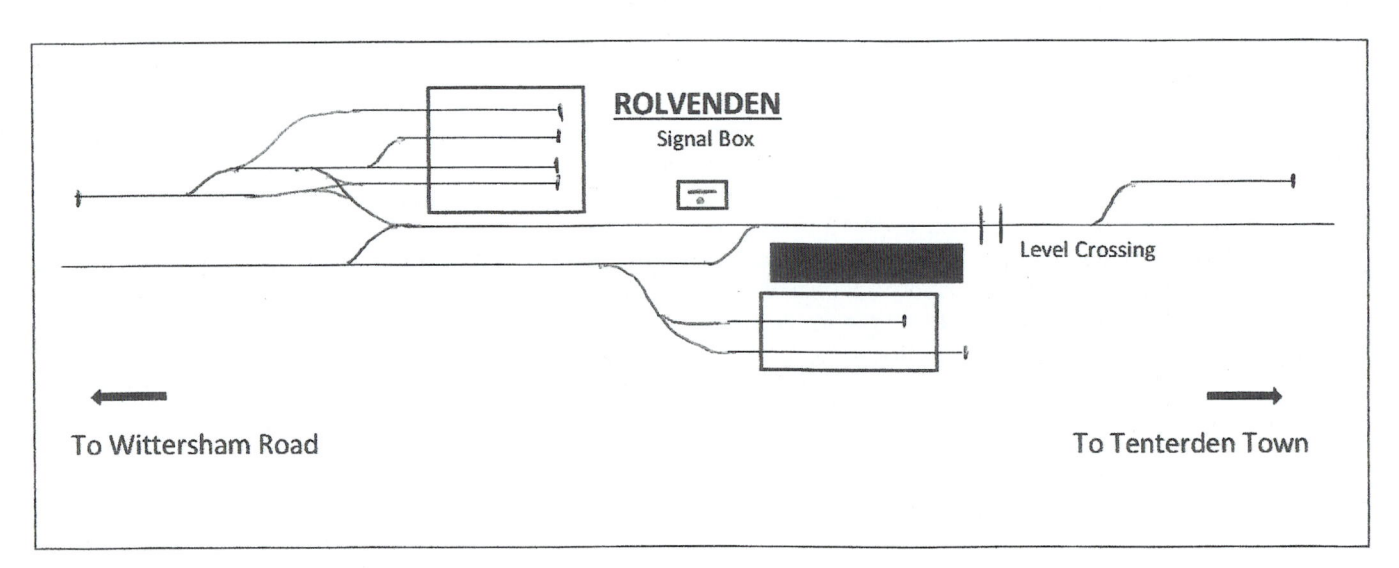

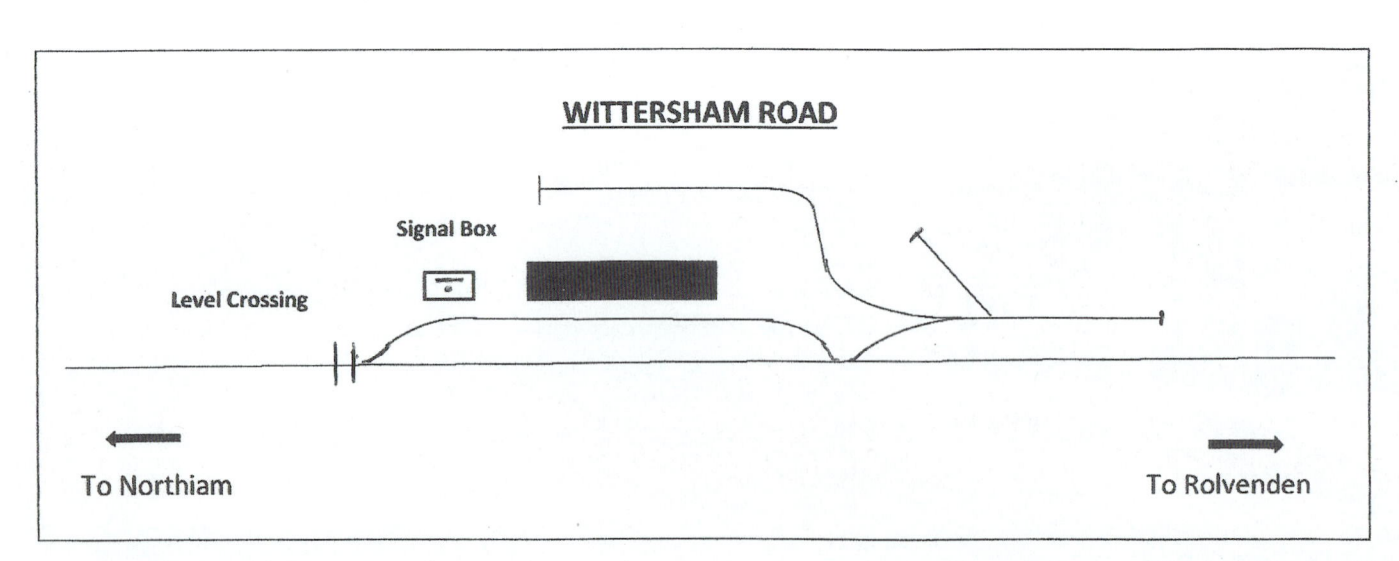

TENTERDEN TOWN

Signal Box
Level Crossing
← To Rolvenden

ROLVENDEN

Signal Box
Level Crossing
← To Wittersham Road
→ To Tenterden Town

WITTERSHAM ROAD

Signal Box
Level Crossing
← To Northiam
→ To Rolvenden

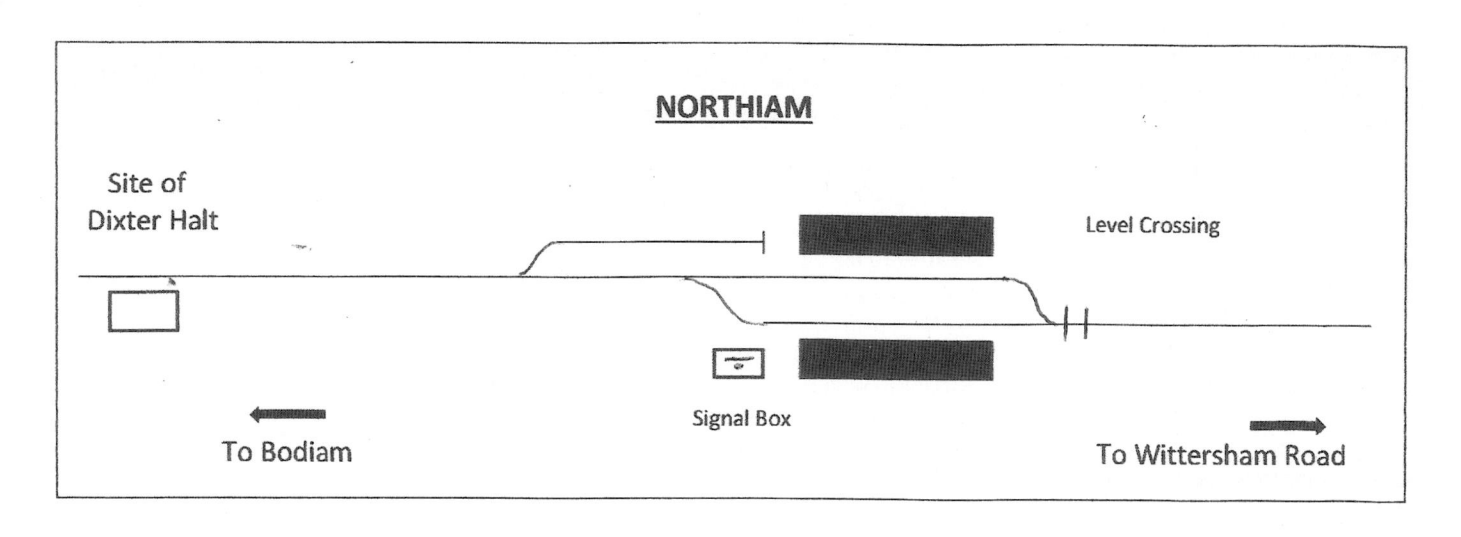

NORTHIAM

Site of Dixter Halt

Level Crossing

Signal Box

← To Bodiam

To Wittersham Road →

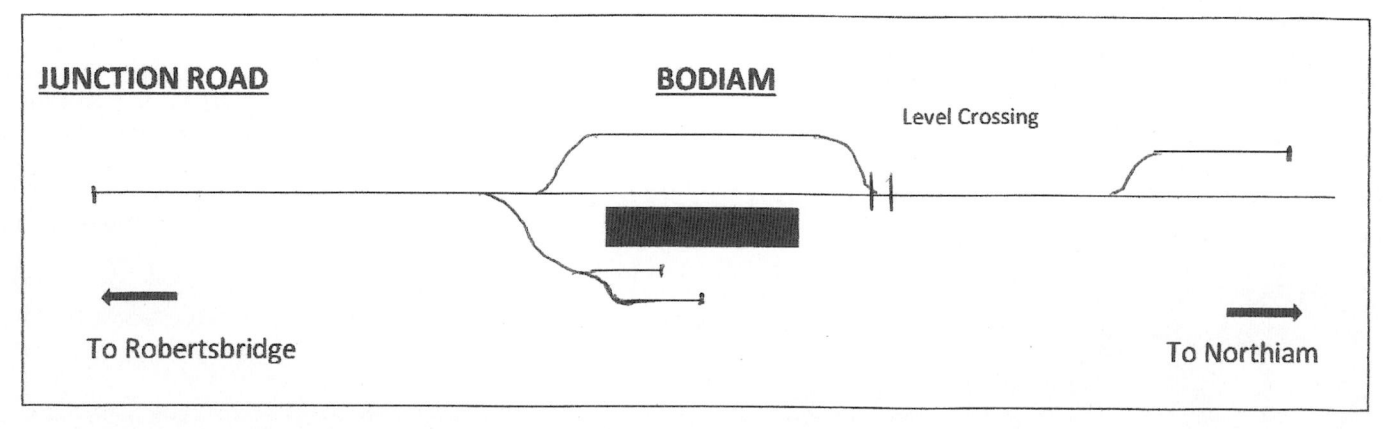

JUNCTION ROAD   BODIAM

Level Crossing

← To Robertsbridge

To Northiam →

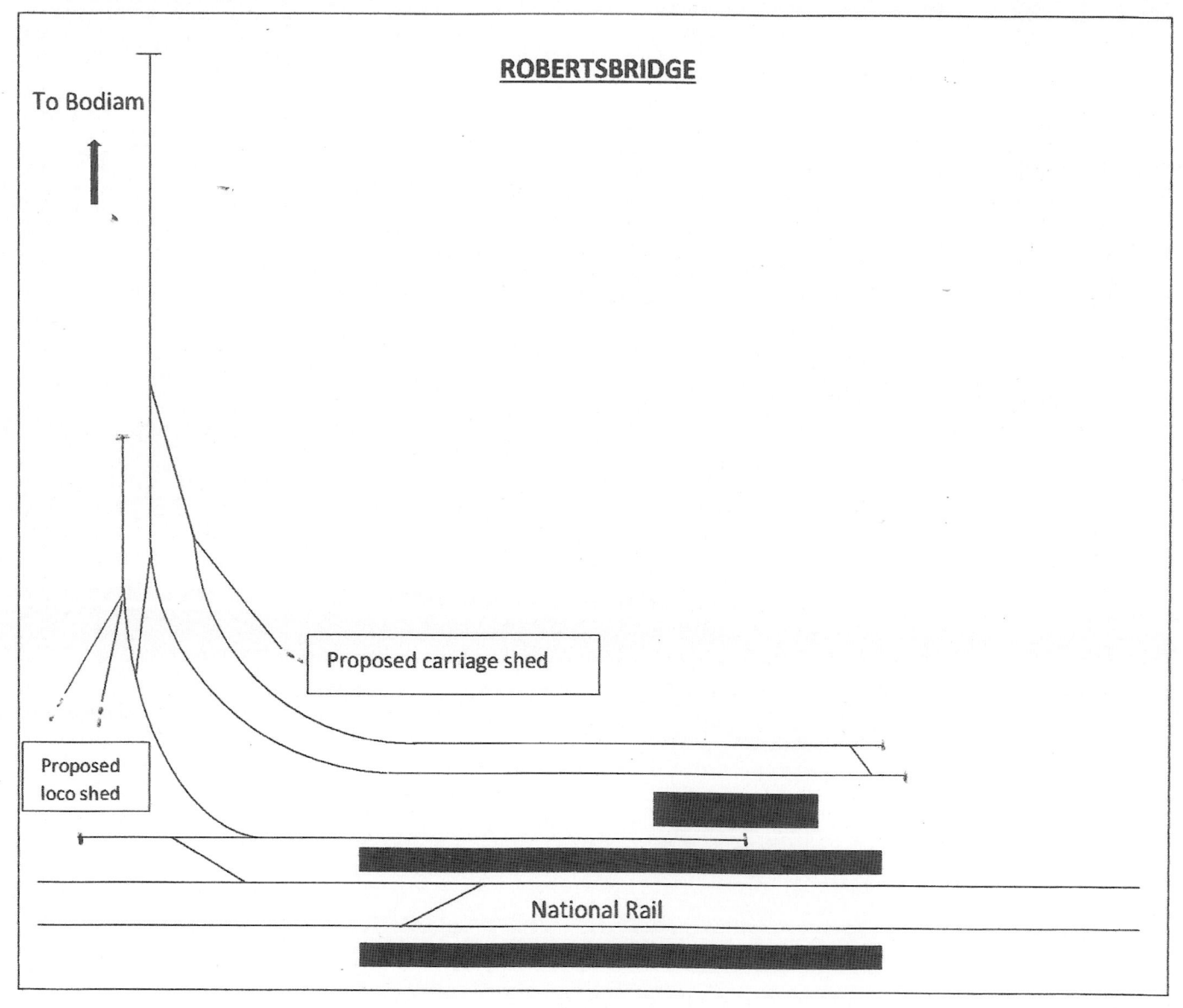

ROBERTSBRIDGE

To Bodiam ↑

Proposed carriage shed

Proposed loco shed

National Rail

A TRIP ALONG THE LINE

Most passengers start their journey at Tenterden, often referred to as the 'Jewel of the Weald', with its fine selection of shops and old buildings.

Tenterden Town station is located just off the High Street and is the headquarters of the Kent and East Sussex Railway. The station has a single platform along with an excellent restaurant and gift shop. The restaurant is located in the former Maidstone bus station building, which was relocated to Tenterden after closure.

The main carriage and wagon works are located alongside the station as well as the Colonel Stephens Railway Museum. There are also some storage sidings where the 'Wealden Pullman' carriages are usually stabled when not in use on the dining train.

The line's shunt neck extends a short distance towards Tenterden St Michael's and the abandoned route to Headcorn.

The approach to Tenterden Town station seen on 17 July 2016.

Jonathan James

A view of Tenterden Town station and signal box on 22 September 2013.

The main station building at Tenterden Town, which houses the ticket office and gift shop, on 17 July 2016.

Both: Jonathan James

A view of Tenterden Town signal box on 5 May 2014.

Pullman vehicle 'Barbara' is seen here in the sidings at Tenterden Town on the same date.

Both: Phil Barnes

The Wealden Pullman carriages and the restaurant building seen on 17 July 2016.
Jonathan James

After leaving Tenterden Town the railway climbs towards Cranbrook Road level crossing. Just before reaching Rolvenden there is a siding which is used to store rolling stock.

As with Tenterden Town, there is a level crossing adjacent to Rolvenden station. Rolvenden is home to the locomotive sheds and workshop, which sit behind the station building.

The station has a single platform, with a passing loop just beyond the platform, which enables trains to pass on busy days. There is also a water tower and signal box.

The rural nature of the railway is evident from this view of Cranbrook Road level crossing, seen here on 17 July 2016.
Jonathan James

The station building at Rolvenden, which retains its' rural charm', seen here on 17 July 2016.
Jonathan James

Shortly after leaving Rolvenden a four-road carriage shed has been constructed in preparation for the extension of the railway to Robertsbridge, providing much needed additional undercover stabling capacity.

The next stop is Wittersham Road, which is the base for the permanent way team. The station has a single platform and a passing loop, meaning that on busy days some trains are unable to call at the station. There is a signal box located adjacent to a level crossing at the Northiam end of the station.

The line was extended from Rolvenden to Wittersham Road in 1977, with the station opening in 1978.

A view of the station and engine sheds at Rolvenden on 17 July 2016.
Jonathan James

The new carriage shed at Rolvenden under construction on 22 September 2013.

Jonathan James

Track laying has commenced in this photograph taken on 5 May 2014.

Phil Barnes

The completed shed seen on 23 May 2015.

Phil Barnes

Class 14 locomotive number D9504 standing outside the completed shed on 17 July 2016.

Jonathan James

A view of Wittersham Road permanent way yard on 17 July 2016.

The signal box and station building at Wittersham Road seen on 17 July 2016.

Both: Jonathan James

After leaving Wittersham Road the railway continues towards Northiam, crossing another level crossing just before Northiam station. Northiam has two platforms and a short siding, as well as a water tower, signal box and cafe. The station reopened in 1990, shortly after appearing on the TV show 'Challenge Anneka', which involved the TV personality Anneka Rice helping with constructing the extension.

From Northiam, trains continue towards Bodiam, with views across the valley towards the famous Bodiam Castle and vineyards. There is a short siding before reaching Bodiam, which is used to store carriages awaiting restoration.

For a short period of time a station was provided at Dixter Halt, adjacent to Great Dixter House, which was used for a shuttle service to Bodiam. It opened in 1981 and was used on an occasional basis until 1983.

As with the other stations on the line, there is a level crossing just before Bodiam station is reached. Bodiam has a single platform, loop, water tower and a couple of sidings. Bodiam station reopened in 2000 when services were extended from Northiam.

Beyond Bodiam, the railway continues for nearly a mile, almost to the site of Junction Road station. This extension was constructed by the Rother Valley Railway and opened in 2011, although it is only currently used for special events.

There are no immediate plans to re-open the station at Junction Road.

Northiam station seen on 17 July 2016.

Jonathan James

The signal box at Northiam seen on 22 September 2013.

The Class 108 DMU waits in the platform at Northiam, also on 22 September 2013.

Both: Jonathan James

Bodiam station, looking towards Robertsbridge, seen in the summer of 1996 before the return of regular passenger services.

A view of Bodiam Castle seen from a train on 22 September 2013.

Both: Jonathan James

Another view of Bodiam station in summer 1996.

A train heads away from Bodiam on 28 August 2004.

Both: Jonathan James

Two views of the carefully restored station building at Bodiam, seen on 17 July 2016.

Both: Jonathan James

The South Eastern and Chatham Railway 'Cavell Van', built at Ashford Works in 1919, is on display in the siding at Bodiam; seen here on 3 July 2011. In 1919 it was used to convey the bodies of Edith Cavell and Charles Fryatt, who were killed in the First World War. In 1920, it carried the body of The Unknown Warrior from Dover to London prior to a funeral service at Westminster Abbey on 11 November 1920. The wagon was fully restored in 2010 and tells the story of the wagon and the three people that it carried. It is seen here on 3 July 2011.

Both: Phil Barnes

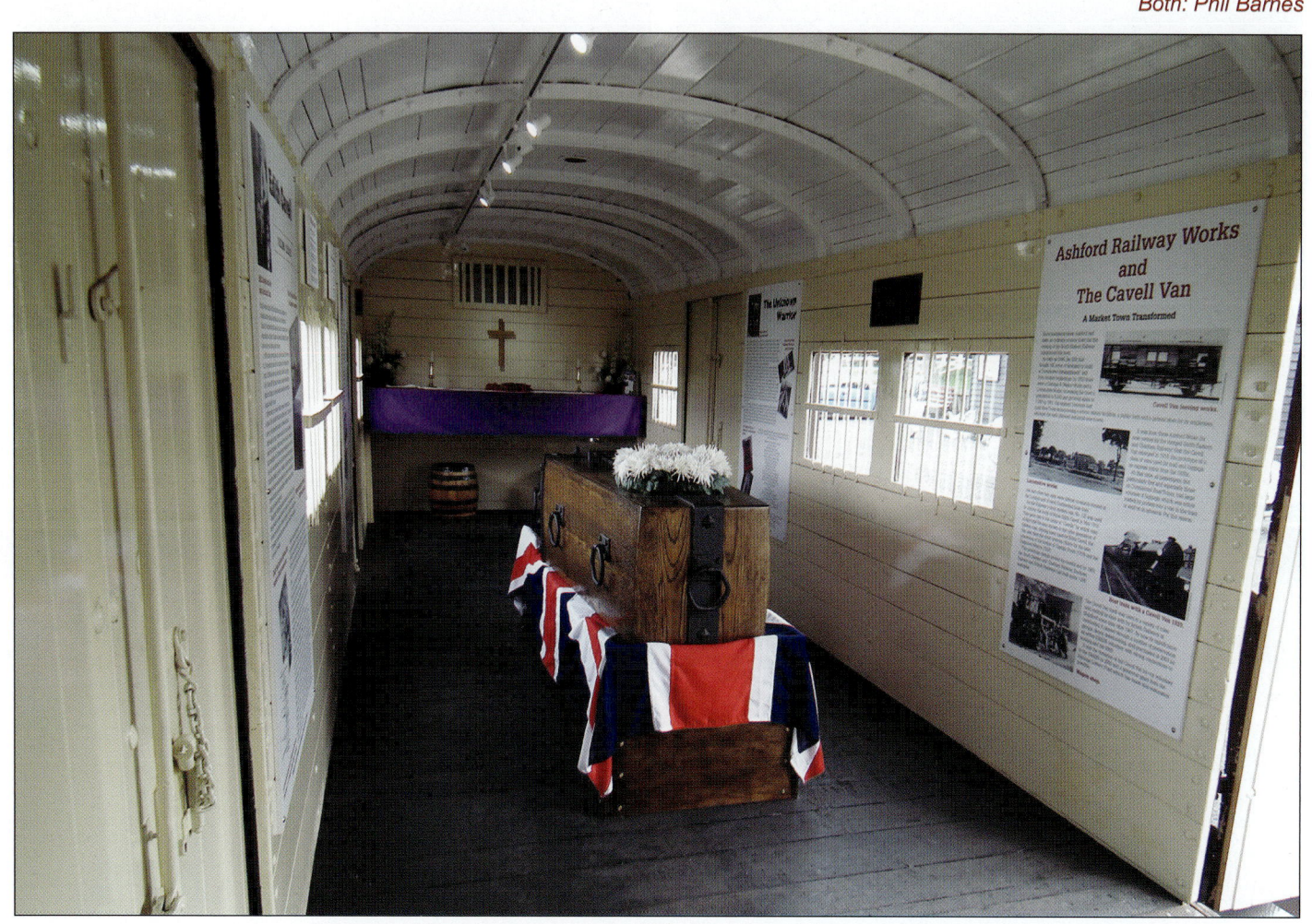

'USA' tank 30065 waits for departure time at Bodiam on 17 July 2016.

Two views along the extension to Junction Road, which stops just short of the former level crossing at Junction Road, seen on 22 September 2013. The level crossing will be reinstated when the line is extended to Robertsbridge, although there are no immediate plans to reopen the station at Junction Road.

All: Jonathan James

ROLLING STOCK

Being constructed as a light railway, the infrastructure was only designed to support smaller locomotives, although since preservation the opportunity has been taken to upgrade the original railway where possible. The locomotive fleet therefore consists of locomotives with a lower axle weight.

Steam Locomotives

Name	Number	Builder	Type	Built	Comments
Bodiam	3	LBSCR (32670)	0-6-0T	1872	A1 Class 'Terrier'
Pride of Sussex	11	SECR (753)	0-6-0T	1909	P Class (1556)
Knowle	8	LBSCR Brighton (32678)	0-6-0T	1880	A1 Class
Frank S. Ross	300 (WD1960)	Vulcan Ironworks (DS237-30070)	0-6-0T	1943	USA Previously called DS238 Wainwright
Maunsell	22	Vulcan Ironworks (30065)	0-6-0T	1943	USA
	1638	British Railways	0-6-0PT	1951	GWR 1600 Class
	4253	GWR	2-8-0T	1917	GWR 4200 Class
	5668	GWR	0-6-2T	1926	GWR 5600 Class
	6619	GWR	0-6-2T	1928	GWR 5600 Class
Marcia	12	Peckett (1631)	0-4-0T	1923	
Charwelton	14	Manning Wardle (1955)	0-6-0ST	1917	
	376	Nydqvist & Holm AB (1163)	2-6-0	1919	Norwegian
Holman F. Stephens	23	Hunslet (3791)	0-6-0ST	1952	Austerity
Northiam	25	Hunslet (3797)	0-6-0ST	1953	Austerity

ST = Saddle Tank T = Side Tank PT = Pannier Tank

Diesel Locomotives

Name	Number	Builder	Type	Built	Comments
	20 (W20W)	GWR	Railcar	1940	Flying Banana
	D2023	British Railways	0-6-0DM	1958	Class 03
	D2024	British Railways	0-6-0DM	1958	Class 03
Dover Castle	D3174 (08108)	British Rail	0-6-0DE	1955	Class 08
	08888 / D4118	British Rail	0-6-0DE	1962	Class 08
	D9504	British Rail	0-6-0DH	1964	Class 14
	D7594 (25244)	British Rail	Bo-Bo	1964	Class 25
Ashford	D6570 (33052)	Birmingham Carriage & Wagon Works	Bo-Bo	1961	Class 33
	51571 / 50971	British Rail	DMU	1959	Class 108
	40	British Thompson Houston (BTH) Company	Bo-Bo	1932	
	41	Ruston Hornsby (423661)	0-4-0DE	1958	

DE = Diesel Electric DH = Diesel Hydraulic DM = Diesel Mechanical DMU = Diesel Multiple Unit

GWR Pannier Tank No.1638, preparing to depart from Bodiam with the 11:45 to Tenterden Town on 3 July 2011.

No.12 Marcia in the sidings at Tenterden Town on 2 May 2011 during the Spring Gala.

Both: Phil Barnes

CSRE Ltd
TENTERDEN
TN30 6HE

*** CARDHOLDER COPY ***

P:W3452005 T:****9440
M:**63462
06/08/2022 17:34:42

Debit Mastercard
************8086

ICC CP SALE

Please debit my account
AMOUNT   GBP102.50
TOTAL   GBP102.50

PIN VERIFIED

Please Keep This Receipt
For your Records
Auth Code: 111373
Ref: Default/011/00072520
AID: A0000000041010
App Seq: 00

Col Stephens Railway Enterprises Ltd
TENTERDEN
Kent
TN30 6HE
01580 765155

06 Aug 2022 17:35
Till No.011/ 111   Receipt No: 11/72520

Qty	Description	Price	Total
1 x	Stephensons Rocket	39.95	39.95
1 x	Electric Drive	45.00	45.00
1 x	K&ESR POSTCARDS	0.60	0.60
1 x	The Kent and East Sussex Rail	16.95	16.95

SubTotal   102.50

                                 102.50

 dit/Debit Card
*********8086

n served by: EL
4.26
27-90

OR YOUR CUSTOM
website at
.org.uk

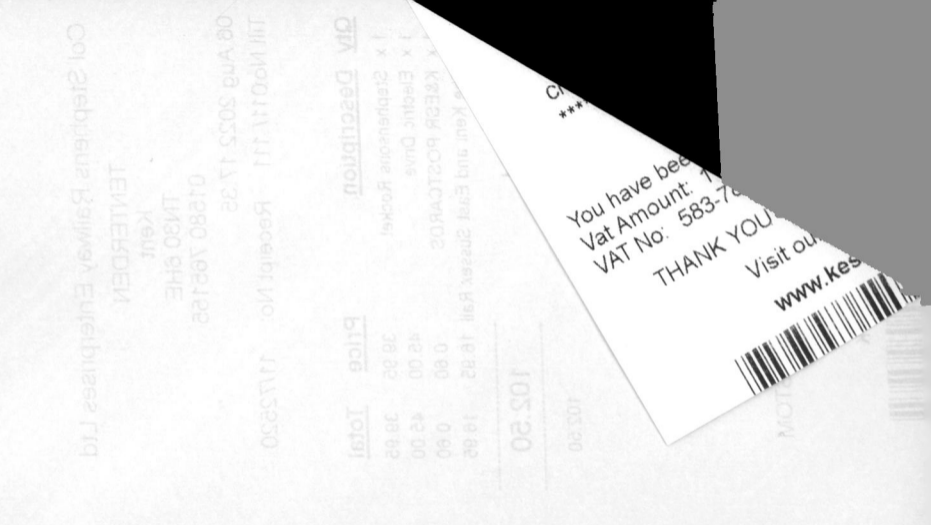

Stephanie Enterprises Ltd
TENTERDEN
Kent
TN30 6HE
01580 765165

Till No:01/1/1 08 Aug 2022 17:35

Description	Qty	Price	Total
Stephenson Rocket	1	39.95	39.95
Electric Drive	1	45.00	45.00
	1	0.60	0.60
KESR POSTCARDS	1	16.95	16.95
Kent and East Sussex Rail			

Receipt No: 1172520

Total 102.50

C...
***

You have bee...
Vat Amount:
VAT No: 583-7...

THANK YOU

Visit ou...

www.kes...

USA Tank DS238 Wainwright and No.14 Charwelton at Tenterden Town on 25 July 1998, during the Loco Cavalcade at 10am.
Phil Barnes

No.14 Charwelton at Tenterden Town on 22 September 2013.
Jonathan James

Two views of No.25 Northiam at Bodiam on 1 September 2001.

Both: Jonathan James

No.23 Holman F. Stephens at Bodiam on 10 May 2019.

No.23 Holman F. Stephens arriving at Tenterden Town on 10 May 2019.

Both: Mike Smith

DS238 Wainwright (WD1960) in War Department livery seen in the siding at Rolvenden on 2 May 2011.

Phil Barnes

DS238 Wainwright at Northiam on 28 August 2004.

Jonathan James

No. 376, the Norwegian locomotive, at Tenterden Town on 17 July 2016.

No.376 running light engine from Rolvenden to Tenterden Town, also on 17 July 2016.
Both: Jonathan James

P Class No. 753 at Bodiam on 4 June 2002 working the 12.15 departure to Tenterden Town during celebrations to mark the 50th anniversary of the reign of Queen Elizabeth II (not 50 years since her Coronation).

The same loco, numbered Southern Railway 1556, heads a short demonstration goods train on 25 October 1997.

Both: Phil Barnes

The P Class, now liveried as ROD 5753, approaches the platform at Wittersham Road. It will shortly couple on to the rear of the 15:50 shuttle service to Northiam, which will be worked 'top and tail'. This was a special working as part of the Spring Gala celebrations on 2 May 2011.

Phil Barnes

30053, an ex- LSWR locomotive built in 1905, visiting from the Swanage Railway, seen at Bodiam on 23 May 2015.

30053 seen at the bottom of Tenterden Bank on the same date.

Both: Phil Barnes

'USA' tank Maunsell, carrying SR livery as 65, at Tenterden Town on 3 July 2011.

Phil Barnes

Another view of the same loco, now numbered 30065 in British Railways livery at Bodiam on 17 July 2016.

Jonathan James

31

Rother Valley Railway liveried 32670 Bodiam, running light engine, at the bottom of Tenterden Bank on 3 May 2009.

32670 Bodiam and 32678 Knowle, top and tailing a birdcage coach, whilst working the 09:30 Tenterden Town to Bodiam, at the bottom of Tenterden Bank on 2 May 2011.

Both: Phil Barnes

32678 Knowle and 14 Charwelton at Northiam on 22 September 2013.

32678 Knowle in the yard at Rolvenden on 28 August 2004.

Both: Jonathan James

33

No.32650 Sutton seen at Tenterden Town on 1 September 2001. This locomotive is now located at the Spa Valley Railway.

Linda (as Thomas) outside the new sheds at Rolvenden on 17 July 2016. The locomotive has since moved to the Mid Hants Railway.
Both: Jonathan James

34

The BTH locomotive and D3174 (08108) Dover Castle at Tenterden Town on 1 September 2001.

The BTH locomotive in the siding outside Rolvenden on 22 September 2013.

Both: Jonathan James

Class 03 D2023 working the late running 17:15 Tenterden to Bodiam mixed train, rounding the curve at the bottom of Tenterden Bank on 3 May 2009.

D2023 arriving at Wittersham Road with the 12:35 freight from Tenterden Town on 23 May 2015.

Both: Phil Barnes

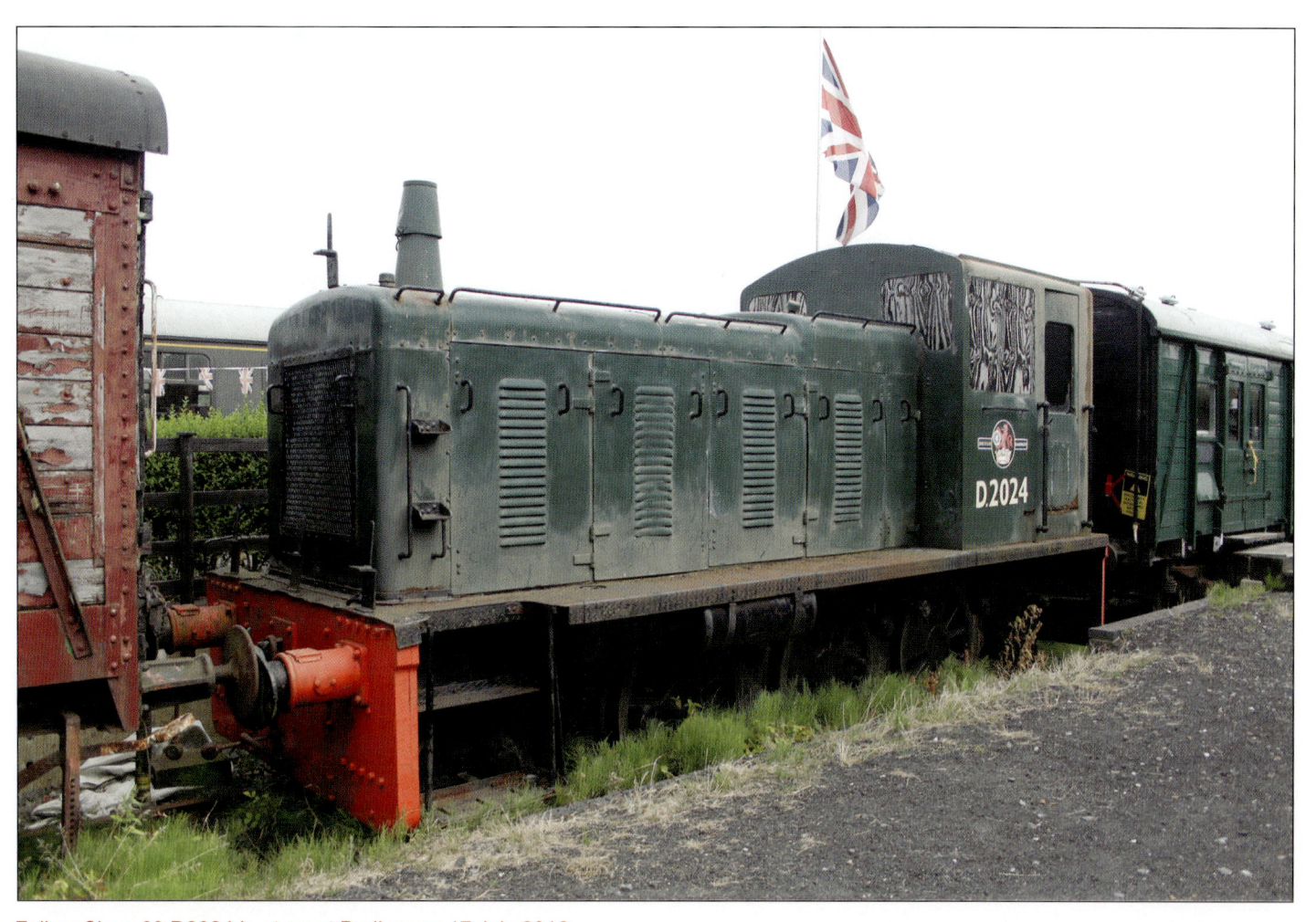

Fellow Class 03 D2024 in store at Bodiam on 17 July 2016.

Jonathan James

08888 climbing Tenterden Bank with the 11:45 Rolvenden to Tenterden Town during the Winter Diesel Gala on 16 January 2000.

Phil Barnes

Class 14 D9504 at Tenterden Town on 22 September 2013.

Jonathan James

D9504 crossing the A28 at Northiam whilst working the 14:30 from Tenterden Town, during a Diesel Running Day on 27 June 2010.

Phil Barnes

A visiting Class 27 locomotive number D5401 arriving at Rolvenden with the 11:30 Tenterden Town to Northiam during a Diesel Gala on 27 June 2010.

D6570 (33052) is seen climbing Tenterden Bank with the 13:50 Bodiam to Tenterden Town on 3 May 2009.

Both: Phil Barnes

Ruston 423661 outside the shed at Rolvenden on 17 July 2016.

Jonathan James

Ruston 423661 outside the shed at Rolvenden with No.376 seen on 22 September 2013.

Jonathan James

Ruston 423661 outside the shed at Rolvenden on 5 May 2014.

Phil Barnes

41

We now take a journey along the line with the Class 108 Diesel Multiple Unit, beginning with this view of it running into the platform at Tenterden Town from the headshunt, on 22 September 2013...

Jonathan James

...at Wittersham Road, whilst working the 12:40 Tenterden Town to Bodiam, on 19 May 2002...

Phil Barnes

...at Northiam on 22 September 2013...

Jonathan James

...and finally at Bodiam on 10 May 2019.

Mike Smith

43

GWR Railcar W20W under restoration in the shed at Tenterden Town on 16 June 2019. The visit was by special arrangement.

Hastings Diesel Electric Multiple Unit 1001 was based at the KE&SR between 1993 and the winter of 1995/1996 and is seen here departing from Wittersham Road on 15 October 1995 whilst working the 14:30 Tenterden Town to Northiam.

Both: Phil Barnes

Former Steam Locomotives

Name	Number	Builder	Type	Built	Comments
Sutton	10	LBSCR (32650)	0-6-0T	1876	Now at Spa Valley Railway
Hastings	15	Hunslet (469)	0-6-0ST	1888	Now at Elsecar Heritage Railway
	1618 (31618)	Southern Railway (A618)	2-6-0	1928	U Class. Now at the Bluebell Railway
Rhyl	15	Manning Wardle (2009)	0-6-0ST	1921	Now at Great Central Railway (Ruddington)
Dolobran	16	Manning Wardle (1762)	0-6-0ST	1910	Now at Great Central Railway (Ruddington)
Arthur	17	Manning Wardle (1601)	0-6-0ST	1903	Now at Middleton Railway
Gervase		Manning Wardle (1472)	0-4-0	1900	Now at Elsecar Heritage Railway
Westminster	18	Peckett (1378)	0-6-0ST	1914	Now at Northampton & Lamport Railway
William H.Austen	24	Hunslet (3800)	0-6-0ST	1953	Now at Colne Valley Railway
Linda	26	Hunslet (3781)	0-6-0ST	1952	Now at the Mid Hants Railway
Rolvenden	27	RSH (7086)	0-6-0ST	1943	Now at Embsay & Bolton Abbey Railway
	56	RSH (7667)	0-6-0ST	1950	Now at the Buckinghamshire Railway Centre
Minnie	358	Fox/Walker	0-6-0ST	1878	Now at Mangapps Farm Railway Museum
Met		Hawthorne Leslie (2800)	0-4-0	1909	Now at a private location in South Wales

ST = Saddle Tank T = Side Tank

Former Diesel Locomotives & Multiple Units

Name	Number	Builder	Type	Built	Comments
	W79978	AC Cars	Railbus	1959	Now at the Swindon & Cricklade Railway
	46 (D2205)		0-6-0DM	1953	Class 04. Now at Peak Rail
	49 (D9525)		0-6-0DH	1965	Class 14. Now at Peak Rail
	49 (D9529)		0-6-0DH	1964	Class 14. Now at the Nene Valley Railway
Baglan	41	Bagnall (8377)	0-4-0DM	1962	Scrapped mid-1980s
	1001	British Rail	DEMU (Class 201)	1957	Based on the railway between 1993 – 1996
Dahlech	42	Hunslet (4208)	0-6-0DM	1948	Scrapped 2001
	43	Fowler (4220031)	0-4-0DH	1964	Now at the Swindon & Cricklade Railway

DH = Diesel Hydraulic DM = Diesel Mechanical DEMU = Diesel Electric Multiple Unit

Maunsell Composite Corridor coach number 5618 built in 1931 seen at Tenterden Town on 22 September 2013.

A carriage stabled near Bodiam awaiting restoration on 17 July 2016.

Both: Jonathan James

Pullman carriage Barbara, which was built in 1926 for use on trains between London and Hastings via Tunbridge Wells, seen on 17 July 2016 at Tenterden Town.

Carriage 3062 built in 1888 by the London, Chatham and Dover Railway, seen at Tenterden Town on 17 July 2016.

Both: Jonathan James

Carriage 2947 built by the South Eastern & Chatham Railway at Ashford in 1901, seen here at Tenterden Town on 17 July 2016.

Carriage 27687 built by the London and North Western Railway at Wolverton in 1911, seen at Tenterden Town on 17 July 2016.

Both: Jonathan James

Birdcage Carriage 1100 built in 1910 at Ashford works seen here at Tenterden Town on 17 July 2016.

Great Eastern Railway carriage 197 built in 1887 and ED33 Inspection Saloon built in 1890, seen at Tenterden Town on 22 September 2013.

Both: Jonathan James

RUNNING THE RAILWAY

Timetables

Trains generally operate at weekends from April to October, plus Easter and Tuesdays to Thursdays between May and September and daily during the school summer holidays. The peak service consists of eight return trains from Tenterden Town, with five return services on a majority of other dates. Special timetables operate on special event days.

Fares

Due to COVID-19 special fares apply at the time of writing and tickets must be booked in advance. The adult return fare in 2018 was £18.00 with a family ticket costing £38.00.

Café and Shop Facilities

There is a restaurant at Tenterden Town as well as a gift shop. Some trains also have buffet facilities, which are indicated in the timetable.

Toilet facilities are available at Tenterden Town, Northiam and Bodiam.

Locomotive and Carriage Sheds

There is a carriage shed and stabling sidings at Tenterden Town station.

The main locomotive shed is located alongside Rolvenden station. In recent years a new shed has been built just outside Rolvenden and additional land has been purchased to enable further expansion.

The permanent way department are based in the sidings at Wittersham Road station and there is a siding at Bodiam that is used to stable some rolling stock. There are also separate sidings near Rolvenden and Bodiam for storing spare rolling stock and vehicles awaiting restoration.

Level crossings

There are several footpath and farmers crossings along the line. There are also road crossings at Tenterden Town, Cranbrook Road, Rolvenden, Wittersham Road, Northiam, and Bodiam.

The extension from Junction Road to Robertsbridge will require the reconstruction of three further level crossings at Junction Road, the A21 Robertsbridge Bypass and Northbridge Street in Robertsbridge.

No. 376 is seen in the loop at Tenterdown Town during the line's Silver Jubilee Gala on 25 July 1999.

Phil Barnes

SPECIAL EVENTS

The railway holds a number of special events during the year, including 'Thomas the Tank Engine' events and Santa Specials. A number of special services operate including the prestigious 'Wealden Pullman' dining train as well as evening Real Ale Trains, the Cider Express and Fish and Chip specials. It is also possible to sign-up to a 'driver experience day' and ride on the footplate of a locomotive.

SE&CR No.65, built in 1896, visiting from the Bluebell Railway, seen at Bodiam on 3 May 2009.

Phil Barnes

Two views from the Light Railway Gala on 25 July 1998, both taken at the foot of Tenterden Bank as the locos attack the climb. We begin with Charwelton and No. 23 Holman F Stephens hauling the 10:55 Wittersham Road to Tenterden engineering train.

A little later, DS238 passes the same spot with the 12:15 Northiam to Tenterden mixed train.

Both: Phil Barnes

A 'Driver Experience Day' in progress on 'USA' tank 30065 on 17 July 2016.

No.23 Holman F. Stephens at Tenterden Town working a Santa Special on 23 December 2006.

Both: Jonathan James

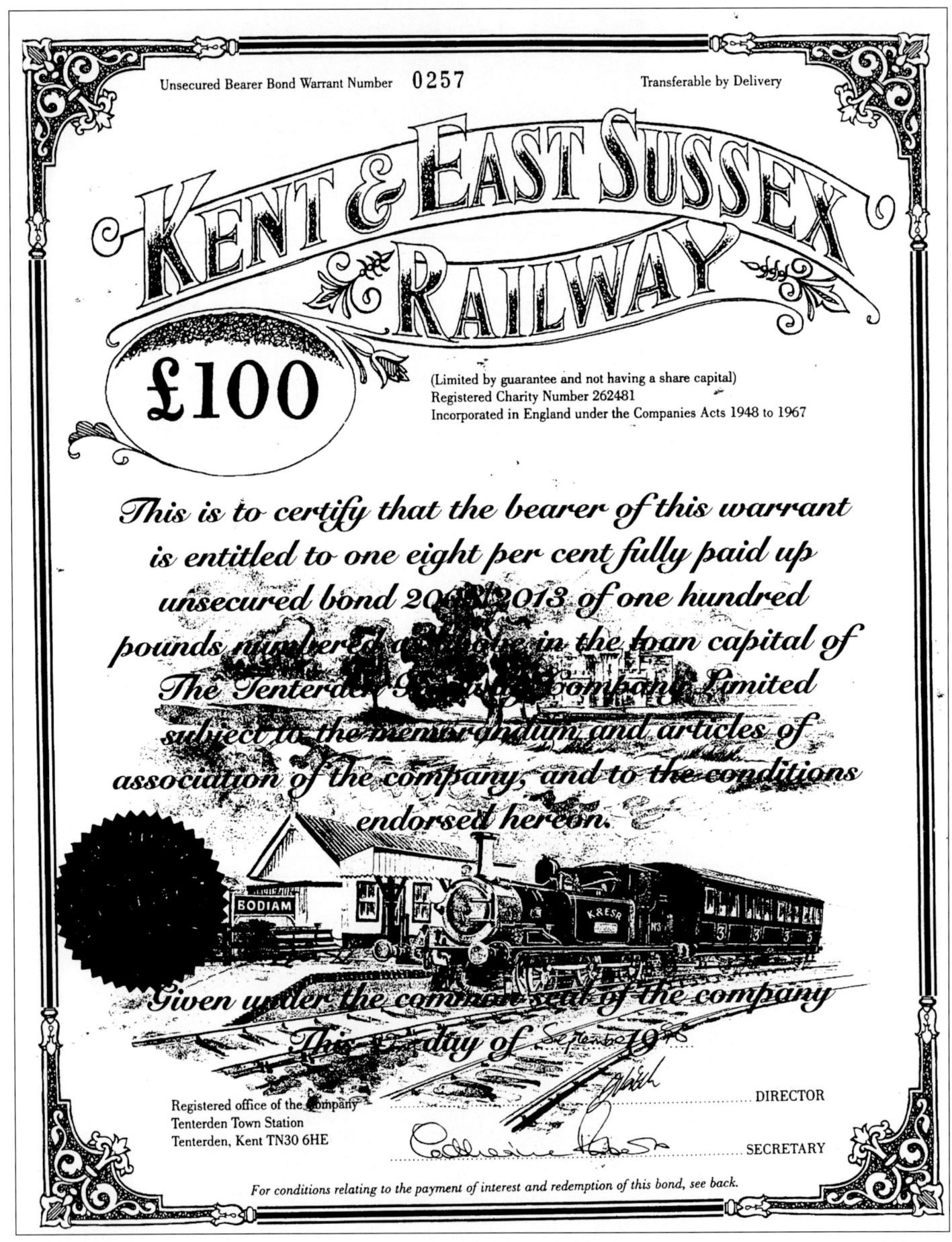

Unsecured Bearer Bond Warrant Number 0257   Transferable by Delivery

KENT & EAST SUSSEX RAILWAY

£100

(Limited by guarantee and not having a share capital)
Registered Charity Number 262481
Incorporated in England under the Companies Acts 1948 to 1967

This is to certify that the bearer of this warrant is entitled to one eight per cent fully paid up unsecured bond 2008/2013 of one hundred pounds numbered as above in the loan capital of The Tenterden Railway Company Limited subject to the memorandum and articles of association of the company, and to the conditions endorsed hereon.

Given under the common seal of the company This —— day of September 19—

Registered office of the company
Tenterden Town Station
Tenterden, Kent TN30 6HE

.... DIRECTOR
.... SECRETARY

For conditions relating to the payment of interest and redemption of this bond, see back.

Phil Barnes

BODIAM 2000 - PROJECT SUMMARY

- Bodiam 2000 is the name of the Kent & East Sussex Railway's project to restore the 3½ miles of line from Northiam to Bodiam. The line will then be a total of 10½ miles long and steam trains will run between Tenterden and Bodiam.

- The Tenterden Railway Co. Ltd. (the registered charity which owns and operates the K&ESR) owns the trackbed and all land necessary for the project and has the requisite train operating licence.

- The total project costs are expected to be £1.95 million. It is hoped to raise up to £500,000 from the Issue of Bearer Bonds - reviving a method used by Victorian Railway entrepreneurs to finance the building of railways.

- Planning and enabling works commenced in 1996 with the production of a business plan as the first step in the application process for a grant from the Millennium Commission. An award of £975,000 was announced in November 1997.

- Other grants have been received from English Partnerships, The European Regional Development Fund, Rother District Council, Ashford Borough Council, Tenterden Town Council and Northiam Parish Council. To date the total value of grants is approximately £1.25 million.

- Key Stages:
    - Removal of worn-out track
    - Clearance of the trackbed and fencing
    - Relaying track at Bodiam Station
    - Rebuilding 35 culverts (pipes taking drainage channels and ditches under the track)
    - Construction of the trackbed
    - Completing the second platform and constructing a Gift Shop at Northiam Station.
    - Rebuilding the platform and restoring the station building at Bodiam
    - Tracklaying and ballasting

- Bodiam Castle is owned by the National Trust and attracts more then 180,000 visitors per year.

- The extension of services will enable the line to provide a "Park and Ride" service from Tenterden and Northiam to Bodiam Castle - alleviating the congestion that occurs on the village lanes in the Summer.

- The target date for the completion of the work is the line's centenary - 2nd April 2000.

If you would like to help ensure trains return to Bodiam for the Millennium, please invest in this exciting project. Copies of the Prospectus are available from the Station Masters at Tenterden Town Station and Northiam.

Phil Barnes

CENTENARY DAY - 2nd April 2000
FEATURING INAUGURAL SERVICES ON THE
MILLENNIUM EXTENSION TO BODIAM

Welcome to the Kent & East Sussex Railway and thank you for joining us aboard one of the inaugural services on our "Millennium Extension" to Bodiam. Passenger services to the station resumed this morning, exactly 100 years after the first train steamed in from Tenterden and some 46 years since British Railways operated the last scheduled passenger train.

Moves to save and restore the line began in the 1960s and the completion of the Bodiam 2000 project will turn the dreams of the line's volunteers, staff and supporters into reality. The project has taken 2½ years to complete, cost £2 million and cleared the last hurdle on Thursday 23 March when the final inspection from the Health & Safety Executive was successfully passed.

The Kent & East Sussex Railway was originally built under the direction of Colonel Holman F. Stephens and made only very meagre profits initially. Road competition in the 20s meant that from 1926 onwards the line incurred ever-increasing losses.

In order to economise Col. Stephens introduced petrol railbuses - these were two road buses linked back to back and fitted with flanged wheels. Although cheap, the buses were rather uncomfortable and were nicknamed "The Bumper" by passengers!

Another unusual feature of the K&ESR was the "Mixed". These were trains formed of 1 or 2 coaches and a string of goods wagons. Running mixed trains was another economy measure - one loco and train crew were used where 2 would otherwise have been required. They were not popular with passengers as shunting of the wagons, sometimes at every station, delayed trains so much that the timetable was often unrecognisable!

Col. Stephens died in 1931 and shortly afterwards the line went into liquidation. Mr. William H. Austen, formerly the Colonel's, assistant was appointed Official Receiver and the railway struggled on until 1939 when the outbreak of war made it an important secondary route to the coast. Materials were diverted via the K&ESR when the mainlines were damaged by bombs.

In 1948 the railway was nationalised and became part of British Railways. Despite improvements, including the re-laying of the track, receipts fell. In a typical week in 1953 only 118 passengers travelled on the 90 trains that ran - most of them empty! The line was closed to passengers in 1954 and the Tenterden - Headcorn section lifted. At the time, Tenterden was the largest town in England without a passenger railway service. The Tenterden - Robertsbridge section was kept open for goods traffic and occasional hop pickers specials until 1961 when that too was closed.

A society was formed to save this enchanting railway and, after a long battle, the section from Tenterden to Bodiam was saved. A two-mile section, from Tenterden to Rolvenden, re-opened in 1974 and thanks to the determination, tenacity and innovation of the line's supporters the line has been extended in stages, culminating today with the resumption of services to Bodiam.

Trains will run daily until September to provide a "Park 'n' Ride" service to the National Trust's famous castle at Bodiam which is just five minutes walk from the restored country station. The Castle attracts over 180,000 visitors every year and we hope our steam trains will help alleviate the pressure on the small country lanes leading to the village. Specially discounted tickets for the train journey and admission to the castle are available from Tenterden Town Station or can be booked in advance by telephoning 01580 766428.

Light Railways

The Light Railways Act of 1896 was designed to encourage the building of railways to rural areas that had been missed in the "railway mania" of the mid-19th Century. Lines could be built more economically as regulations relating to curvature, gradients and fencing were eased, although the maximum speed and weight of the trains were restricted. Light railways were built as cheaply as possible - this often meant stations were several miles from the villages they purported to serve!

The first line to be built under the 1896 Act was the Kent & East Sussex Railway. This was constructed by a railway entrepreneur of the time, Colonel Stephens, who took full advantage of the Act and went on to run an empire of minor lines as inexpensively as practicable. This gave his railways a charm all of their own and much of this delightful atmosphere survives to remind us of an era where the pace of life was less hurried.

Phil Barnes

No. 23 Holman F Stephens stands at Bodiam on opening day, 2 April 2000.

Phil Barnes

KENT & EAST SUSSEX RAILWAY

CENTENARY DAY - 2nd April 2000

Inaugural services on the Millennium Extension to Bodiam

Valid for **THIRD CLASS** travel as detailed below

Train departs from TENTERDEN TOWN STATION

at ......3.20pm......

Coach ......C...... Seat No. ......13......

Fares as advertised   Not transferable
Available only on the date and train shown
Issued subject to the conditions and regulations of the Tenterden Railway Co. Ltd.

Phil Barnes

The BTH Ford locomotive is at Tenterden Town in primer during the Diesel Gala on 16 January 2000. The locomotive was confined to station limits due to remedial work being required to the tyres on the locomotives' wheel sets.

The BTH locomotive at Northiam, with the 11:37 shuttle from Bodiam, during the Diesel Gala on 19 May 2002.

Both: Phil Barnes

The Great Western comes to Kent as 0-6-0PT 1638 pilots the iconic 3717 City of Truro on a light engine move from Rolvenden to Tenterden at the start of the operating day on 2 May 2011.

Visiting French replica locomotive 'Marc Seguin' at Tenterden Town during the 25th Anniversary Event on 25 July 1999.

Both: Phil Barnes

Terrier locomotives 662, No.3 Bodiam and No.32678 Knowle rounding the curve at the bottom of Tenterden Bank whilst working the 16:50 Bodiam to Tenterden Town on 3 May 2009, during the 'The Last Train's Gone' Gala.

No.662 Martello built in 1875, visiting from Bressingham Gardens, working the 13:52 Wittersham Road to Tenterden Town engineers train during the 'The Last Train's Gone' Gala on 3 May 2009.

Both: Phil Barnes

SE&CR No.65, built in 1896, seen at Bodiam on 3 May 2009.

No.65, visiting from the Bluebell Railway, seen at the "The Last Train's Gone" Gala, working the late running 15:25 Wittersham Road to Tenterden "demolition train", rounding the curve at the bottom of Tenterden Bank on 3 May 2009 .

Both: Phil Barnes

COLONEL STEPHENS RAILWAY MUSEUM

The Colonel Stephens Railway Museum is located opposite the station platform at Tenterden Town, alongside the carriage shed. The museum charts the life of Colonel Holman Fred Stephens, who was responsible for the construction and management of 16 light railways, including the Kent & East Sussex Railway. He was also involved in a number of other railways in the Kent, including the East Kent Railway, Rye and Camber Tramway, Sheppey Light Railway and the Hawkhurst Branch. Entry to the museum if free although donations are appreciated. The museum contains a wide variety of artefacts as well as a bookshop.

Locomotives

Name	Number	Builder	Type	Built	Comments
Gazelle	1	Dodman & Co	0-4-2WT	1893	On Static display. On loan from the National Railway Museum

Left: A truck from the Ashover Light Railway, another Colonel Stephens line, on display at the museum on 17 July 2016.
Jonathan James

Right Upper: No.1 Gazelle, dating from 1893, on display inside the museum on 16 June 2019
Phil Barnes

Right Lower: A replica of a Ford Railbus that once operated on the railway, seen on 16 June 2019.
Phil Barnes

Left: A Rye and Camber carriage frame seen on 17 July 2016.
Jonathan James

HATHERLEIGH
PRIVATE PROPERTY
NO ADMITTANCE TO THE RAILWAY IS PERMITTED
BEWARE OF TRAINS
HALWILL
PLEASE DONATE
To help maintain this locomotive
33
32
L.C.G.B.
LIMITED.

RAILWAY MUSEUM
WEIGHED DOWN BY LOOSE CHANGE?
All donations go towards the restoration of our Vintage Carriages

THE ROTHER VALLEY RAILWAY

The Rother Valley Railway is a separate organisation to the Kent and East Sussex Railway, which has the specific aim of rebuilding the railway line between Bodiam and Robertsbridge. Around a mile of track has been laid between Bodiam and just short of the level crossing and station site at Junction Road.

At the Robertsbridge end of the line a new station has been constructed alongside the national rail station, along with five bridges and around a quarter of a mile of track between Robertsbridge and Northbridge Street. Work has started on clearing the land already owned by the Rother Valley Railway, whilst awaiting the outcome of a Transport and Works Act application covering the remainder of the route. Planning permission for the extension has already been granted, but there is considerable work to complete, including three level crossings and the remainder of the new station building at Robertsbridge.

Once completed, through trains will operate over the Rother Valley Railway and Kent and East Sussex Railway between Robertsbridge and Tenterden Town.

Locomotives

Name	Number	Builder	Type	Built	Comments
Titan	D140	Drewry/Vulcan (2279)	0-4-0DM	1951	
Dougal	D77	Drewry (2251)	0-4-0	1947	
	D2112 (03112)	British Rail	0-6-0DM	1960	Class 03
Telemon	No.1	Vulcan (D295)	0-4-0DM	1955	Now at the Cambrian Railways Society

DM = Diesel Mechanical

The end of the line at Northbridge Street seen on 7 July 2013.

Jonathan James

The route between Robertsbridge and Northbridge Street before the bridges were replaced and the route restored, seen on 20 March 1999 during a public open day.

Phil Barnes

The end of the line at Northbridge Street seen on 7 July 2013.

Jonathan James

Class 03 'Ford No.4' leading a demonstration freight train at Robertsbridge on 20 March 1999.

D2112 at Robertsbridge on 2 September 2018.

Both: Phil Barnes

D2112 at Robertsbridge on 22 September 2013.

Jonathan James

2-EPB No.5793 was stored at Robertsbridge for a time, but is now located at the Battlefield Line, see here on 20 March 1999.

Phil Barnes

No.3 Bodiam, carrying British Railways livery as 32670 between Northbridge Street and Robertsbridge on 22 September 2013.
Phil Barnes

32670 arriving at Robertsbridge station on 22 September 2013.
Jonathan James

The new trackwork taking shape at Robertsbridge on 2 September 2018. The connections will eventually lead to a locomotive shed.
Phil Barnes

32670 operating a shuttle service between Northbridge Street and Robertsbridge station on 22 September 2013.
Jonathan James

Titan and D77 are seen in a line of other rolling stock in the sidings at Robertsbridge on 2 September 2018 .
Phil Barnes

D77 (2251) at Robertsbridge on 22 September 2013.
Jonathan James

No.1 Telemon at Robertsbridge on 1 September 2001.

Titan at Robertsbridge seen on 22 September 2013.

Both: Jonathan James

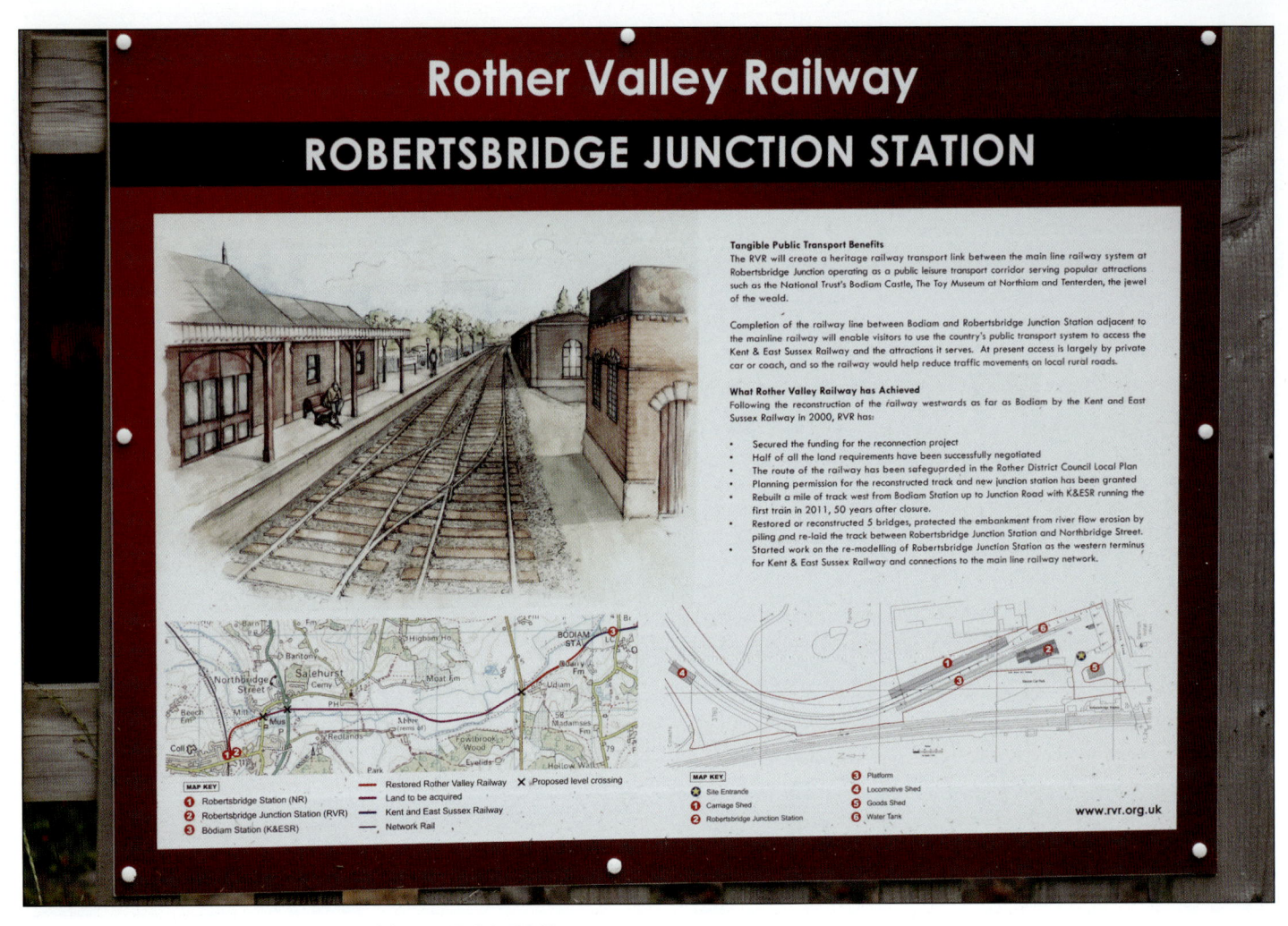

The station display board at Robertsbridge on 7 July 2013.

The Rother Valley Railway Museum building at Robertsbridge seen on 7 July 2013.

Both: Jonathan James

The new station at Robertsbridge under construction on 7 July 2013.

Jonathan James

The new station at Robertsbridge taking shape on 2 September 2018.

Phil Barnes

32670 arriving at Robertsbridge from Northbridge Street on 22 September 2013.

A view from 32670's train arriving at the new Robertsbridge station on 22 September 2013.

Both: Jonathan James

The Rother Valley Railway Museum at Robertsbridge on 7 July 2013.

Jonathan James

PUBLICITY MATERIAL

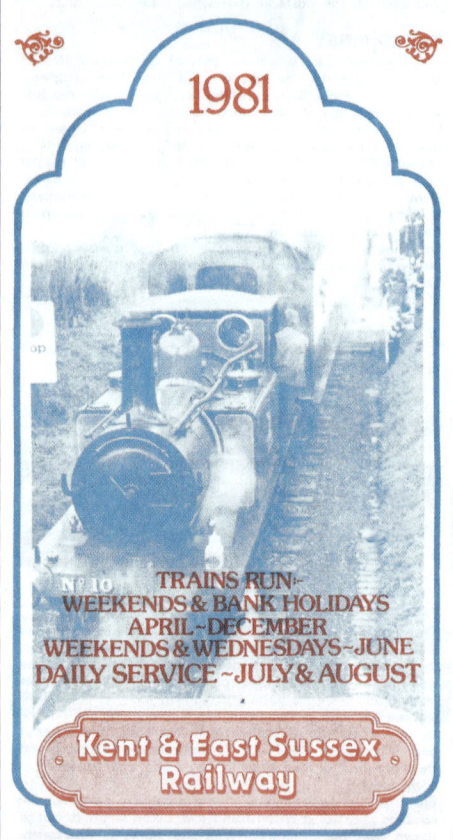

STEAM TRAINS AT TENTERDEN

1981

N° 10 — TRAINS RUN:
WEEKENDS & BANK HOLIDAYS APRIL~DECEMBER
WEEKENDS & WEDNESDAYS~JUNE
DAILY SERVICE~JULY & AUGUST

Kent & East Sussex Railway

Kent & East Sussex RAILWAY

STEAM TRAIN SERVICES
JANUARY TO DECEMBER 1992

TIMETABLE & INFORMATION

Kent & East Sussex Railway
Tenterden Town Station
Tenterden · Kent TN30 6HE
Telephone: (05806) 5155

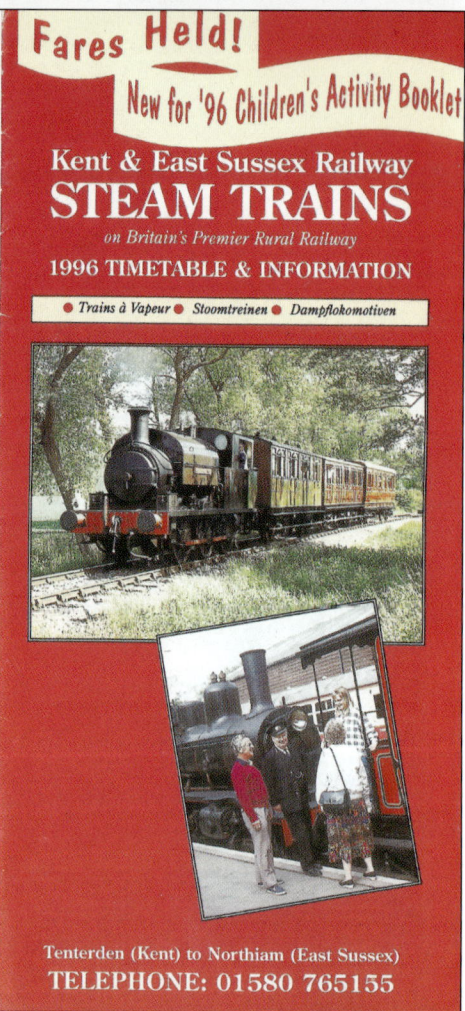

Fares Held!
New for '96 Children's Activity Booklet

Kent & East Sussex Railway
STEAM TRAINS
on Britain's Premier Rural Railway
1996 TIMETABLE & INFORMATION

- Trains à Vapeur • Stoomtreinen • Dampflokomotiven

Tenterden (Kent) to Northiam (East Sussex)
TELEPHONE: 01580 765155

Kent & East Sussex Railway
Steam Trains
on Britain's Premier Rural Railway
1997 TIMETABLE & INFORMATION

- Trains à Vapeur
- Stoomtreinen
- Dampflokomotiven

Pay once & TRAVEL ALL DAY

Tenterden (Kent) to Northiam (East Sussex)
TELEPHONE: 01580 765155

KENT & EAST SUSSEX RAILWAY
TENTERDEN ~ NORTHIAM ~ BODIAM
1900 – 2000

3½ MILE EXTENSION OPENS APRIL

April to September
STEAM TRAINS EVERY DAY

2000 TIMETABLE & INFORMATION
TALKING TIMETABLE
FREEPHONE 0800 9800 923

A MILLENNIUM PROJECT
SUPPORTED BY FUNDS FROM THE NATIONAL LOTTERY

KENT & EAST SUSSEX RAILWAY
Tenterden–Northiam–Bodiam 1900–2001

One of the UK's longest, oldest and most popular full-size light railways

SPECIAL EVENTS 2001

TIMETABLE & SPECIAL EVENTS

Steam trains daily from 5th May to end of September. Reduced service at other times.
Talking timetable: Freephone 0800 9800 923
Enquiries: 01580 765155

ON-LINE ENTERTAINMENT

A MILLENNIUM PROJECT
SUPPORTED BY FUNDS FROM THE NATIONAL LOTTERY

KENT & EAST SUSSEX
STEAM RAILWAY
TENTERDEN • NORTHIAM • BODIAM
TIMETABLE 2003
Tenterden Town Station Centenary
1903 – 2003
TENTERDEN TOWN STATION
TENTERDEN KENT TN30 6HE
01580 765155
www.kesr.org.uk
VISITOR ATTRACTION

Kent & East Sussex Railway
Kent & East Sussex Railway
Timetable & Guide 2007
M
Millennium Commission
G W R
England's finest rural light railway

Kent & East Sussex Railway
Timetable & Guide 2008
NEW events for 2008
M
England's finest rural light railway

TENTERDEN – NORTHIAM – BODIAM
Kent & East Sussex
Railway
Timetable and
Guide 2009
M
NEW events for 2009
England's finest rural light railway

TENTERDEN – NORTHIAM – BODIAM
Kent & East Sussex
Railway
2010 Timetable
and Guide
No fare increase this year!
32678
England's finest rural light railway

TENTERDEN – NORTHIAM – BODIAM
Kent & East Sussex
Railway
2011 Timetable
and Guide
New For 2011
The Cavell Van · The Mill Toy Museum
England's finest rural light railway

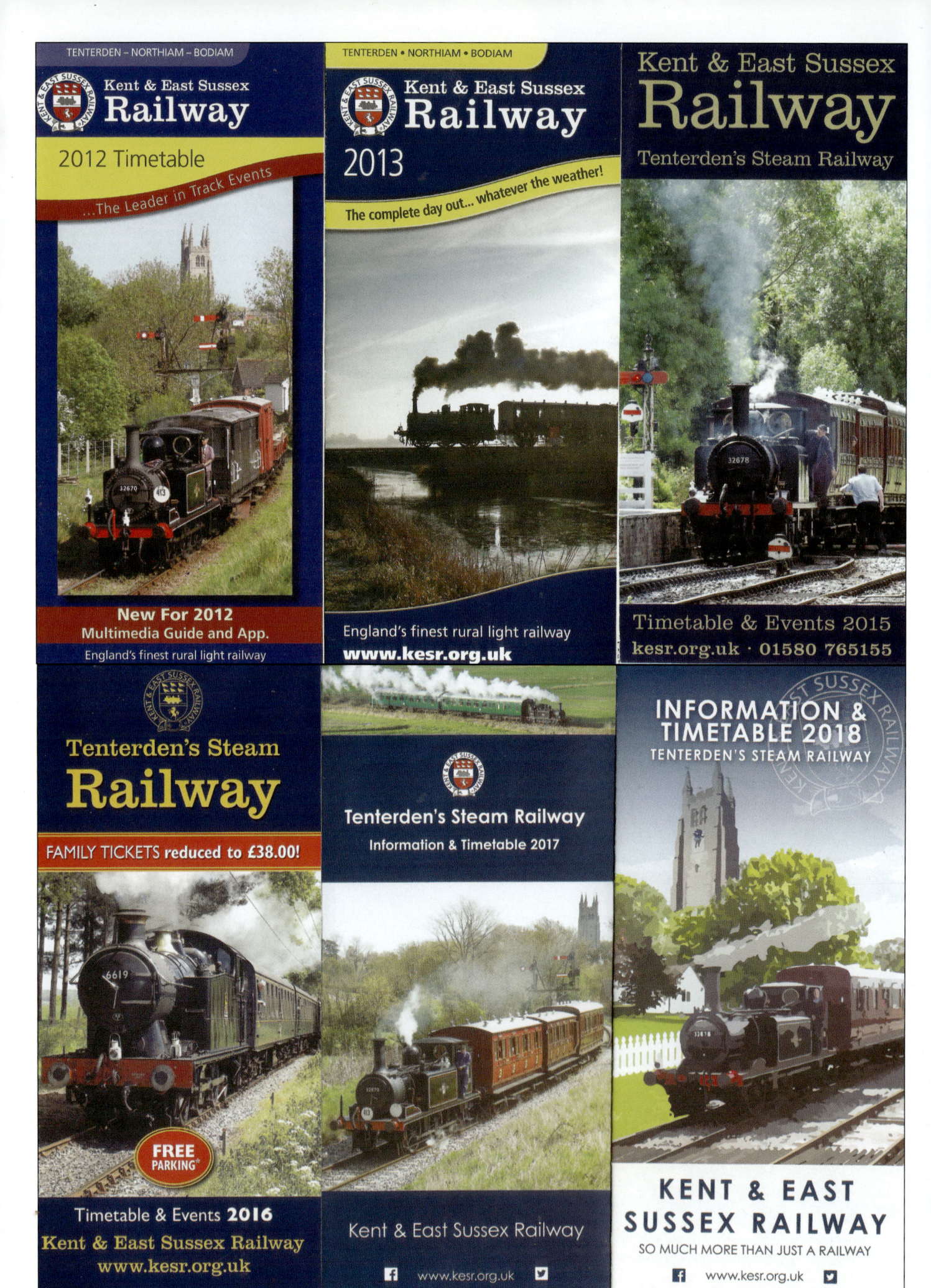

Visit The Colonel Stephens Railway Museum

Heritage Railway Magazine MUSEUM OF THE YEAR 2014

- See the Colonel in his faithfully reconstructed Tonbridge office in the 1920s with original furniture

- Marvel at the world's smallest standard gauge loco *Gazelle*, built in 1893

- Tour the many displays, and study the models, photographs, nameplates and other preserved items from the railways he managed

- Watch fascinating short videos telling the story of his railway empire, including a newsreel of one of his innovative but notorious Ford railmotors

- Learn about the Stephens family and its Pre-Raphaelite artistic background

- Sit in a carriage typical of those that ran on the Colonel's lines

Rother Valley Railway

ROBERTSBRIDGE STATION
STATION ROAD
ROBERTSBRIDGE
EAST SUSSEX

(ADJACENT TO MAIN LINE STATION)

OPEN EVERY SUNDAY &
BANK HOLIDAY
0930 – 1700
(or Dusk if earlier)

Kent & East Sussex Railway
Return to Robertsbridge

Robertsbridge Station is set to echo to the distinctive sights, sounds and smells of steam as the re-opening of the **Rother Valley Railway (RVR)** between Robertsbridge and Bodiam takes a major step forward.

Saturday 21 and Sunday 22 September, 2013

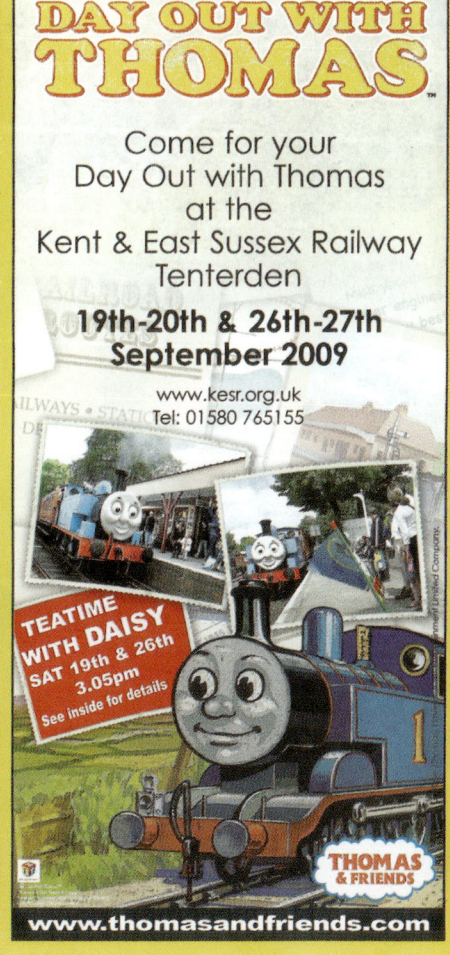

TENTERDEN • NORTHIAM • BODIAM

Kent & East Sussex Railway
Welcome...
The complete day out... whatever the weather!

England's finest rural light railway
www.kesr.org.uk

DAY OUT WITH THOMAS

Come for your Day Out with Thomas at the Kent & East Sussex Railway Tenterden

19th-20th & 26th-27th September 2009

www.kesr.org.uk
Tel: 01580 765155

TEATIME WITH DAISY
SAT 19th & 26th
3.05pm
See inside for details

THOMAS & FRIENDS
www.thomasandfriends.com

Kent & East Sussex Railway
Tenterden Town Station

Our famous Santa Specials

Our 39th Year Of Festive Fun

Book Early - www.kesr.org.uk

England's finest rural light railway

SELECTED FURTHER READING

Title	Author	Publisher
Branch Line to Tenterden	Vic Mitchell and Keith Smith	Middleton Press, 1985
Britain's Heritage Railways	Andy Chard	Platform 5, 2019
Holding the Line – Preserving the Kent and East Sussex Railway	N Pallant	Alan Sutton Publishing, 1993
Lost Railways of Kent	Leslie Oppitz	Countryside Books, 2003
The Kent & East Sussex Railway Guide	Simon B. Green	Tenterden Railway Co.Ltd, 1974
Stockbook – The Locomotives and Stock of the Kent & East Sussex Railway	Alan Dixon and Donald Wilson	Tenterden Railway Co.Ltd
The Kent & East Sussex Railway Stockbook	Neil Rose	Colonel Stephens Publications (K&ESR), 1984
The Kent & East Sussex Railway	Stephen Garrett	The Oakwood Press, 1987
The Kent & East Sussex Railway Guide	Simon B. Green	Buffer Stop Books,
The Kent & East Sussex Railway Colour Guide	Graham Hukins and Mark Toynbee	Kent & East Sussex Railway, 1990
The Kent & East Sussex Railway	Terry Gough	Past & Present Publishing Limited, 1998

376 runs round the loop at Bodiam as it prepares to haul the 14:43 to Tenterden on 5 May 2014.

Phil Barnes